SOMETHING I MIGHT SAY

SOMETHING

I MIGHT SAY

STEPHANIE AUSTIN

wtaw
press

Edited by Peg Alford Pursell
Designed by Amit Dey
Cover photograph courtesy of the author.

Library of Congress Control Number: 2023938324
Austin, Stephanie
Something I might say / Stephanie Austin
ISBN: 978-1-7336619-5-9 (pbk) | ISBN: 978-1-7336619-6-6 (ebook)

Published by WTAW Press
PO Box 2825
Santa Rosa, CA 95405
www.wtawpress.org

WTAW Press is a not-for-profit literary press. We are grateful for the assistance we receive from individual donors, public arts agencies, and private foundations.

For Cecilia

CONTENTS

SOMETHING I MIGHT SAY

October 2019

MY FATHER, ON HIS DEATHBED, asked if I had any regrets about our relationship. The cancer had taken most of his voice, so all he could do was whisper, "Regrets?" I tossed my head back and laughed. I said, "Oh my God, Dad." I laughed again. I did not, and do not, have regrets. Well, I suppose I regret that I cannot put this scene in a story because it is a cliché. (Who tosses their head back anyway?) And I regret mailing the bitter letter I wrote to him before I attended his second wedding, when I was twenty-one.

His deathbed was a hospital bed. Thank you, hospice, for bringing the bed, the drugs, the nebulizer, the counselor, the medicated mouthwash for thrush.

A technicality: We were in the living room where the bed was set up because there was more space, and I was sitting on the hospital bed, his deathbed, and he was sitting in his walker, which had a warning label that read, DO NOT USE AS A SEAT. I towered over him, my dad, small and hollow, without hair or teeth. Once six four and 220 pounds, he was hunched over from the lung cancer eating up his chest cavity, his feet and ankles swollen with fluid buildup. Fluid is part of the body's defense system. The body fights to the end. The body opts for hope.

The two of us were alone. The day caregiver was down the hall, maybe in the bathroom. The 24-hour caregiver group I'd hired was expensive, but hospice offered a volunteer for only a few hours and my father, who had little time left, could not be alone. I worked a full-time job an hour away. I also had a four-year-old, and my extended absences at home were noticed. In the beginning, I'd tried to bring my daughter with me to my dad's, but small children require all the attention in the room. They get bored. The last visit, she couldn't stop jumping back and forth over his oxygen tubing. I needed to put motherhood aside, however impossible, and focus on him.

My father wanted his patio doors open. It was October in the desert, finally cool enough in the mornings and evenings to allow this.

Years earlier, he stopped washing or trimming his hair, slicking it back with oil instead. It had grown long and scraggly and yellowed, and I was embarrassed both by and for him. After he began chemo, his hair had fallen out in patches. I'd bought him a lint roller to help catch the strands. I was not sorry to see that hair go.

"Dad," I said, "listen. You are you, and I am me, and we are who we are because of separate and shared circumstances. No regrets."

He nodded. I patted his hands, which were warm. The hospice literature told me the extremities may be cold. I read all the literature hospice brought: Give the gift of comfort and calm. Give them support, permission. Give them more than they gave you.

I always tell the dress story, a microcosm of my father's transgressions: He took me shopping for my freshman-year high-school homecoming dance. I did not have a date. No one had asked me. I was going with friends. Boys did not like me. They thought I was weird, and I probably was weird. The problem was how much I liked boys, how much I needed their attention.

We lived in Lake Havasu, Arizona. Our town had a Walmart and a Kmart. The pretty girls had their parents drive them to Vegas or Phoenix to buy clothes. My dad took me to a strip mall in town where a shop sold off-brand girls' clothing. I wanted a Jessica McClintock dress. *Seventeen* magazine advertised Jessica McClintock dresses, so I believed a Jessica McClintock dress was the key to boys and popularity. The shop did not sell Jessica McClintock dresses.

I tried on a blue cotton dress with pink flowers. This was the 1990s, when girls wore prints with big flowers on their dresses. I had a weight problem that wouldn't go away for another two years and wore a size 12.

I came out of the dressing room, and my dad looked me over.

"Maybe if you ate apples instead of cookies that dress would look better on you," he said.

New drinking game: Every time your dad destroys your self-esteem, take a shot. Every time someone laughs at the story of how your dad destroyed your self-esteem, take a shot. Every time the story falls flat, take a shot. Find the bad men and tell them the dress story. Listen to them say your dad sounds like an ass. Agree and laugh. Laugh and laugh and laugh. *What a fucking asshole.* Take a shot.

Join Team Mom. Dad is the reason they got divorced. Feel it in your body: Dad's fault. Dad hurts everything he touches, including himself.

Everyone who entered my father's house in Phoenix had to look at the wooden triangles he'd arranged and positioned at odd angles like an abstract painting on the wall outside his bedroom. He'd made them from pieces of an old chair; the vintage wood looked used. He would point to the shapes and ask what we could see.

"Christ, I don't know, Dad. Triangles? Your woodworking skills?"

He'd shake his head. "Look closer." My dad was into puzzles: not putting them together but making them. My dad was his own puzzle.

He never told me what the triangles meant.

After my daughter was born, while I was going through postpartum depression, I spent hours online "researching" child development. My sister was slow. What if my child might also be slow? I needed to know as soon as possible, for the sake of early intervention. I watched for the signs of typical development, for her to roll front to back, then back to front; to sit up, speak, wave, and clap; to make eye contact. *Make sure the baby looks you in the eye,* I read. *Make sure the baby smiles.* She smiled for the first time at three weeks and continued to hit the rest of her milestones on time, to my relief.

Maybe the emotional disconnect I felt with my father—that most people felt with my father—was not his fault. I asked his siblings: "What was my dad like when he was young? Did he have friends? Did he make eye contact? Tell me about his eye contact."

He was kind of a "strange bird," I was told. He "had his own way," and that way was not often cute or charming. As he grew older, his way was heavy drinking, long periods of isolation, and saying what he thought without regard for other people's feelings.

No one had ever diagnosed him with autism, but he could have checked every box on the list of symptoms I'd found online. I'm not saying he had autism. I'm saying he fit all the criteria. I'm saying that believing he had a processing issue was the only way I could open a space for forgiveness.

Summer break from college, 1998. I was at my dad's house waiting for my boyfriend to call. I took the cordless phone off the cradle and made sure it worked. I moved the phone from the countertop to the kitchen table as though that might make it ring. My boyfriend knew I was back in town and still he had not called nor returned any of my phone calls.

"What are you doing?" my dad asked.

I was being desperate and sad, but I could not let my dad know this. Maybe this weekend my boyfriend and I would go out to dinner, hold hands in public. Maybe this weekend he might acknowledge me as his girlfriend.

My father was waiting for an answer. "My boyfriend—" I began.

"Boyfriend?" he said. "Who is he?"

I told him the boy's name and a little about our relationship.

"He's your *boyfriend*?" my dad asked again.

Did I need to spray-paint it on the wall? Boyfriend. Boy. Friend.

"He doesn't sound like a boyfriend, if he only calls once a month."

"You do not get to tell me who is or isn't my boyfriend, Dad. I know."

My mother and I had already discussed this. She'd said my dad had been the same way when they were dating. Distant. Calling only when he felt like it, or when he wanted something. Partying. Going out with other women. She said this had continued into their marriage.

But they *had* gotten married, I pointed out to her. So, there was hope.

She reminded me that her marriage to my father had imploded. They'd been divorced longer than they'd been married.

My dad repeated, "I do not think he is your boyfriend if he doesn't call." In his way, he was telling me to expect better for myself. This guy was not treating me well. My father's own actions showed me otherwise, and I could not reconcile the two.

Small-cell lung cancer. Aggressive.

My father and I sat in the waiting room before his first oncology appointment. The cancer center waiting room was full of travel magazines: Got cancer? Go to Belize!

My dad motioned for me to lean closer. He told me it was not important for the doctor to know he had smoked almost his entire life. (He was sixty-nine.) He said it would not matter, that lung cancer was lung cancer. He did not want to be judged. (I already judged him.) He said he planned to tell the doctor he had quit smoking more than two decades ago.

During the exam, the doctor pulled up my father's lung scan and said his lungs looked like the lungs of a person who'd smoked for fifty years. My dad remained stoic. The doctor said he was not judging, but my dad's self-reported history did not match what he saw on the scan. My dad said nothing. I said nothing. The doctor ran down a list of my father's ailments, including stage-3 COPD—chronic obstructive pulmonary disease.

(After the appointment, I asked, "Dad, how long have you had COPD?"

"About ten years," he said.

"Ten years? You had that diagnosis ten years ago?"

"My GP told me she suspected it, but I should get it confirmed. I never did. Didn't matter.")

The doctor said he was surprised my father wasn't on oxygen. My dad was often out of breath and used oxygen at night, as a result of a sudden hospitalization a few years earlier for alcoholic hepatitis. I'd found out about the oxygen only because the supply company had called me one afternoon when they could not get in touch with him.

When I was growing up in the 1980s, my dad was a laborer. He wore flannel shirts and trucker hats and always smelled like sweat, cigarettes, and beer. My dad had a friend named Stan, and we would all go to Stan's house out in the woods in rural Illinois. This area was thick with trees, which seemed like a jungle, and was full of small lakes and rivers. Stan had a dog named Ribs, or maybe Bones. Something to do with the skeleton. He lived beside a lake edged with sand, but my sister and I were not allowed to walk barefoot there so we wouldn't cut our feet on broken glass. My dad and Stan drank beer and built things together. My father surrounded himself with other alcoholics.

Stan died in a drunk-driving accident. His car slid off an icy backroad and into a tree. My mom said Dad was drunk at the funeral. He situated a six-pack of beer and a hammer in Stan's casket, angering Stan's sister who asked him to leave.

"Stan liked beer," my dad said in defense. "I want to send him off with something he liked."

My dad sent me a text. He had thrown up in the car on the way to his radiation treatment.

I knew to expect this. Chemo makes you sick. But I had questions. I texted back: *Threw up, like, you were sick and you threw up? How did you throw up?*

He texted: *I threw up.* He'd used a cup of water to wash off the seats. He said he tipped the valet at the cancer center ten dollars. He usually gave the guy three dollars but vomit got him ten dollars.

I needed to know the circumstances in which the throwing up had happened. Sudden? Succumbed to prolonged nausea? A lot? A little? Just once or did he throw up twice? *Was it twice, Dad?*

At his next oncology appointment, I encouraged him to tell the nurse about the vomiting. She asked the same questions I had. His blood pressure was low. His skin was white. He said he'd been having trouble swallowing and sometimes choked on food.

(Our conversation when the nurse stepped out of the room:
"How long have you been choking on food?" I asked.

8

"A few months."

"A few *months*?"

"I'm in decline," he said. "I've been in decline for a long time.")

The doctor explained to him that food sometimes went into his lungs because the mechanism in the throat that directs food had lost function. The mechanism got confused and sent food into the lungs, causing aspiration pneumonia.

"Maybe this is it," Dad said when he realized he couldn't eat. "Maybe I'm done."

His eyes went red and watery, but no tears fell.

I patted him on the shoulder. I asked if he wanted to keep going, if he wanted to have hope. He said yes.

The solution for people who can't swallow is a feeding tube inserted through their side into the stomach. My dad would get formula for nutrition, like an infant. The doctor also gave my father swallowing exercises to do, so that when he got better—when the massive tumor inside his chest disappeared from the radiation, and if the radiation itself did not cause permanent damage—he could get off the feeding tube and start eating again.

Oncologists are the most hopeful people.

———

Once, my father left me a scathing, drunk voicemail. "How dare you?" he shouted. "What right do you have?"

I had left him a message first. I'd told him, via his answering machine, my sister, at age 25, had officially been diagnosed with Mild Mental Retardation as classified by the DSM-IV. She was also diagnosed as on the autism spectrum.

I'd sent an email to my family with the subject line Mental Retardation. I laid it all out. Here was the reason why she is the way she is. Now we could get resources for her. This was helpful, and I was the savior.

They wrote back to thank me. I deserved to be thanked. I'd taken over. I'd handled it because no one else could. Because that's what I'd always done. That was my role in my family: I handled everyone's problems.

My sister, who had always been slow and different, had not gotten enough attention or assistance in schools or society. In the early 80s, kids like my sister were considered either learning disabled or special ed without nuance. Diagnosis matters. You can't deal with something if you don't know what it is. I'd pushed my mom to get my sister formally tested but hadn't included my father in the discussion. He and my mother didn't get along well, and I hadn't wanted to add anymore tension.

He hadn't responded to the family email, so I'd left him the voicemail. After he heard my message, he got drunk: his go-to fix. When I listened to his drunk voicemail, I cried into my hands. He was angry I'd told our family that my sister had a formal diagnosis. It's no one's business but ours, he said. I cried but knew my dad was wrong for yelling, because I was the hero. I'd done something no one else in the family had. I deserved the love he did not seem capable of giving.

I got drunk. I threw up, and I laughed about it to make sure everyone knew: the poison did not have the same effect on me.

My dad walked around in his house at night, his night caregiver said. He sat down on the couch, got up, walked into his bedroom, laid down, and got up and told anyone who would listen they needed to help him find his car keys because he had to go home.

When he did this with me, I asked where home was, and he wrote down his correct address. I said, "That's where you are. You're at this house right now."

Restlessness comes because the body begins to understand it is dying, but the mind cannot cope.

He tried to cut his oxygen tubing. He said he needed to cut the tubing to breathe. I told him no, it's the opposite. I took the knives from his house. I took the scissors. I drove around with his knives and scissors in my trunk.

One night, the caregiver called and asked me to come over because my dad could not calm down. When I arrived, he was on his hands and knees in the living room. He said he was putting up his defenses. He advised me to protect my family.

He refused the antianxiety pills. I told the caregiver to put the medication in his feeding tube.

In the break between chemo and his first radiation treatment, my dad was hospitalized for ten days to have the feeding tube placed in his stomach. I stopped in to see him after work before going home one evening. The room was gamey—he hadn't showered. But he didn't want his door open. I had my notebook open, jotting notes, as I sometimes did. Like most writers, I had a day job. I worked in commercial real estate. The notes might be for a story I was working on. Maybe his eulogy. Or maybe a playlist for his funeral. I asked him what his favorite album was.

He asked why I wanted to know.

I said I didn't know my father's favorite album. It was a thing I needed to know.

"*Rubber Soul,*" he said.

"The Beatles' *Rubber Soul*?"

"How many *Rubber Souls* are there?"

When I was in high school, my dad and I watched each of the three episodes of the documentary *The Beatles Anthology* together. I loved the Beatles and wanted to go back in time to Shea Stadium and scream until I was hoarse and get trampled to death. My mission, then, was to memorize all the Beatles music, and I asked my dad for Beatles CDs for Christmas. He bought me a Byrds album. He liked The Byrds, he said. They were popular back in the 60s, too. I didn't like the album and later traded it at a music shop for gas money. I put "Turn, Turn, Turn" on his funeral playlist.

One afternoon a few days before he died, I left work early to meet the hospice nurse at his house for her weekly visit. I let myself in and found my dad sitting at the kitchen table. When he saw me, he stood and drew his arm back.

I hesitated. Did he think I was an intruder? Was he going to hit me?

No. He wanted to hug me.

My dad and I were side huggers at best. We sort of stepped into each other's space and patted each other's backs. He often slipped out of family events without saying goodbye to anyone—if he showed up at all.

But now my dad opened his arms to me, and we held each other for a long time, and, yes, here was the moment I'd wanted my whole life.

Autumn in the desert feels like summer to some people, but typically it's a pleasant, calming time of year. The sun is less violent. The days are shorter and the nights cool down. I wore a light jacket early mornings and evenings.

That evening I was home and had left my phone downstairs because I wanted a second of peace. As my father lost his capacity, the caregivers called me at all hours with questions, and I needed a break.

My daughter's bath was almost ready, and I was trying to corral her into the tub. My husband walked into the bathroom holding out my phone. "Hospice," he said.

The nurse on the phone told me my dad had collapsed in his hall bathroom. The caregiver had managed to get him back into his bed, but his breathing was labored, he was confused. The end was likely near, and I should come. I left my husband and daughter in the bathroom and drove.

It was dark when I arrived. A hospice nurse was administering morphine. I stood over his bed. The nurse said my dad had been in pain, it was obvious in his face, but the morphine helped and now he was peaceful.

I touched my dad's shoulder. "Dad?" He opened his eyes, but his brown irises were gone, replaced with milky blue. He turned his head toward me, confused about a sound he could not identify.

"Dad," I said again. "Dad. Dad."

The hospice nurse said he was in the active dying phase. She administered morphine, and his expression grew calm. That was how she knew he was not in pain, she said. It might take up to forty-eight hours, she said, but I should not to be surprised if he died that night.

I called my dad's younger sister, his only sibling in Arizona, and she came over. The caregiver, the nurse, she, and I all sat in chairs in the living room. Was this the vigil? It was 11 p.m. It might be a long night. I wondered if I should get a few hours' sleep in the back room. There was a Murphy bed in there. His bedroom was available, and though the bedsheets were clean, I would not—could not—sleep in his bed. He'd soiled it several times. I could not sleep on a stained mattress. That mattress had to go. I mentally inventoried what else had to go, what could stay, what I wanted or didn't want. But where could I sleep while he died? On his couch? Should I go home to sleep? Did I want to sleep while my dad died next to the caregiver?

The caregiver covered him with a blanket, and he was startled again. His body jerked. He seemed very alive. The caregiver laughed. "Oh, dear, I disturbed him. He didn't like that." I laughed, too. We needed to laugh. She said she'd been doing this for twenty-five years. It had taken five years for her to feel OK about "guiding people to God." That's how she put it. Her job was to guide people out of this life and into the next. She said this like she was giving directions.

Good, because I could not guide my father into the next life. I could not even sit next to him as he died.

What would a good daughter have done? Send the caregiver home? Take over administering the morphine?

I touched his shoulder again. "Dad?"

He turned toward the wall, away from me. I laughed again. My aunt laughed, too. "That's so Dad," I said. "To turn away from me."

"Some people want to be alone," the caregiver said.

Animals crawl away under a bush to die. But he had changed positions as if he were sleeping, as if it was any other night and he was simply uncomfortable for a moment.

I went home at midnight.

It was five when I woke and called the caregiver. My father had passed moments ago. That was the word she used: *passed*. He had tried to get up at one point. He'd sat up, swung his legs around and tried to stand, but she'd guided him back down to the hospital bed. She was the guide, guiding. I was the daughter home sleeping.

The end of the chaos—the end of his life—brought a temporary relief. The back and forth was over. The long calls to the caregivers were over. The rushing out of work in the middle of the day because he was in the hospital and alone and the guilt was too much was over. The nights away from my daughter and husband were over. We could all go back to how we were.

After he died, there was no place for my bitterness about him, about men, about life, to go. No place for my righteous sense of emotional abandonment. My dark, awful feelings had always been directed at him, and now he was gone, and those feelings hovered around me like ghosts.

My dad had a brief second marriage that lasted a few years. He'd called me a few months after their divorce. It might have been a year. We went long stretches without talking.

But this time he wanted to talk. His friend Charlie had died. Charlie and my dad had been hippies together. At fifty-five, Charlie had dropped dead of a heart attack in his home where he'd lived alone.

Dad asked me to meet him at a place he liked near his house called Jack's, where he drank a pitcher of beer and said he was still mad at me over the time I'd told his ex-wife I thought he was an alcoholic. She had used it as a weapon against him when they argued: "Your own daughter thinks you're an alcoholic." Like it was my fault they'd gotten divorced.

I watched people sitting alone at the bar, watched the bartender lean toward them to take their drink orders. I tried to be vague and lighthearted because I do not like confrontation.

"I think you drink too much *sometimes*, Dad," I said into the air, and did not look at him. "I don't remember saying that, though it does sound like something I might say."

———

This is what I know. My father is dead. I am alive. He needed me at the end. I needed him my whole life.

My dad and I enjoyed hiking together. We have the same color of eyes.

He liked Kit Kat bars and strawberry-rhubarb pie. He drank Miller Lite.

He was a heavy drinker. He smoked pot and cigarettes for fifty-five years. Empathy was impossible for him.

His high school buddies sent cards after he died. They spoke of him as a formidable character, a guy with an offbeat sense of humor, a teammate, a friend, a nice person.

I wrote thank-you cards and put them in the mail.

I found his high school ring in a box of empty plastic bottles in the garage. The stone in the ring was loose. It rattled when

I shook it. His high school diploma was water-damaged and moldy. I threw it away.

His couch was stained with dried feeding tube formula. His furniture was all hand-me-downs he had carried with him through a bunch of moves, end tables and shelves he'd made himself, a kitchen table with only three chairs. I donated it all.

I put my dad's senior picture in a frame on my mantle next to his urn. I stared at his young, clean-shaven face and tried to imagine what had broken him.

I found my grandmother's music box, a laminated copy of a letter my grandfather had sent my father, a letter from a doctor who'd examined my sister as a child, a book about lesbian vampires, my grandfather's model airplanes and old Navy hat, hundreds of matchbooks, empty notebooks, Sudoku puzzles, thirty years of tax returns, divorce papers (both rounds). I found the sheet music for *Les Mis* in his desk next to a tin whistle.

In his nightstand, I found a pack of cigarettes stuffed into a sock. I laughed and held them up to my husband. "Jesus Christ," I said. "He lived alone. Who was he hiding these from?"

KILL FLOOR

OCTOBER 23, 2019, SOMETIME BEFORE 6 a.m., pitch-black outside. I needed a tampon. My father was dead. I called my mother because I needed to go to my father's house and I wanted my husband to come with me, so could she please come sit with my daughter who was still sleeping. She said she'd get ready, then she handed the phone to my sister.

"Dad died," I said. I wanted my sister to accept our father not as a father but as a person. I wanted him to have been a better father to both of us. I wanted us to be a family who united in grief. I wanted coffee.

"Okay," she said.

I sent my boss a brief text to say it had happened, he had died. I pulled my hair up, packed a shitload of tampons and ibuprofen, put on a light jacket. My mother arrived, slightly elated. I broke in two. Half went to my mother: a man who ruined her life was gone. Half went to my father: a victim of his own poor choices. A smoker. Lung cancer. My mother used to smoke too.

I told my husband I was ready to leave. I told my mother to call me when my daughter woke up so I could talk to her, so she could know even though I wasn't home again, I was thinking about her. For three months, between a full-time job, a small child, and my father needing more and more care, I'd been absent. I put her to bed each night but still was gone in my mind. You cannot have a conversation with a four-year-old about a sense of duty and grief. My boss responded to my text and told me to take all the time I needed.

My husband drove, and I called my father's brothers and sisters, some of whom answered. They were sad with me. I needed the sadness.

At my father's house, the caregiver shifts changed twice a day, 6 a.m. and 6 p.m. He'd died in the early morning hours between shifts, and the new caregiver arrived unaware. She'd known my dad for the three weeks of his dying, when his entire personality was a raspy voice and card games to pass the time. She hugged me. I peeked around her. The hospice nurse held his wrist in her hand and took his non-pulse. My aunt walked in—I'd left the door open. More hugs. Quiet.

Funeral home bodies are prepared and painted to give the appearance of alive but asleep. Palatable. But this was real death with no cover. No pancake makeup. No nice suit. No hands clasped over his chest. His skin was as white as the bedsheets. My father stretched out on his hospice bed in the living room, in a stained white T-shirt and underwear, one stiff knee up in the air, eyes closed, mouth half open, head cocked back, chest raised as though someone had tied a string around his upper body and tried to pull him up but failed. The hospice nurse was preparing to clean him.

"Honey," said the hospice nurse. "Do you want a moment?"

My aunt dabbed her eyes. My husband leaned against the dividing counter between the living room and the kitchen. Did I want a moment? With my father's dead body? No, I didn't want a fucking moment with my father's dead body. My cramps went to an eleven. "I'm good," I said, turning my head. "I'm good. I'm good. Good." The nurse asked if I was sure. "Good," I repeated.

I went into the kitchen. Hospice, i.e., the project coordinator, had wanted a funeral home on file in order to make the call when the time came. The funeral home staff would show up with a gurney on which they would load my dead father and take him to the crematorium. The hospice nurse let me know they, Waverly Brothers, were on their way. I clutched the edge of the counter and squeezed my eyes shut. Cramps. *Cramps.* After my daughter was born, my period was casual, light. Friendly. After I turned forty, it grew nasty and unpredictable again. Everything swelled. Cramps became a three-ibuprofen-every-four-hours event. It was a kill floor.

I stood at the kitchen counter and then I felt it. A subtle yet obvious gush. A *fuck-you.* I crossed my legs, grabbed my bag, excused myself to the bathroom, but not the hall bathroom because my dad had collapsed there the night before. You can't change your tampon in the bathroom where your dad fell off the toilet and into the tub because the mass in his chest had probably exploded.

In the bathroom, my mouth dropped. I had bled all the way through the tampon, all the way through the pad I'd put in my underwear in case the tampon failed, all the way through my underwear, into my shorts. I peeled off my underwear, shoved them into my purse pocket. The last time I'd bled through to my shorts was in high school. High school was when I'd moved into my dad's house to get away from my stepfather. High school was when my dad had thousands of beers in his fridge that he let me drink on occasion. High school was when my dad and I sort of got okay for a bit.

Then I remembered the laundry basket on the floor outside the bathroom door. My dad had lost so much weight, I'd purchased several pairs of sweatpants and shorts for him. My six-foot-four father who'd once topped off at 220 had worn a baggy men's medium. I found a pair of clean black sweatshorts with a drawstring. An open box of disposable underwear, compliments of hospice, lay on the floor. Heavy absorbency. I put on the disposable underwear and my dad's shorts. I pulled the drawstring up on the cheap shorts and returned to the living room where the Waverlys now waited for me.

They were the tallest men I'd ever met. Their voices were calming, low, as if the living room now full of bright sunlight was theirs. (Why, my dad often asked, would a person spend money on curtains when the natural cycle of the sun was a curtain.) The brothers, the hospice nurse, and the caregiver together lifted my dad from the bed onto the gurney.

The Waverlys asked if I wanted to walk out with the body. Should they pull the sheet back so I could see his face? Please everyone, stop asking me if I want to gaze upon my dead father. The people in my father's retirement community were out walking in the sun. Garage doors were up, golf carts packed. The Waverlys closed the van doors. My husband and my aunt and I, wearing my father's disposable hospice underwear and his black drawstring shorts, stood in the driveway watching the van go until it turned the corner.

My husband gave me a funny look. "Did you change your clothes?" he asked.

"Nevermind," I said.

Inside the kitchen, I removed the magnets that held the orange DO NOT RESUSCIATE (DNR) page to his refrigerator and opened the door like it was time for breakfast. Yesterday, less than twenty-four hours ago, I had filled new droppers with morphine and Ativan. Caregivers were not allowed to set meds, only administer them, and we'd gotten a new shipment. My dad had been in good spirits. We'd sat at the table. The hospice nurse listened to his breathing, wrinkled her nose a bit. After she checked his vitals—which, other than the gurgling lungs, were good and normal— he stood, said he was tired, and laid down on his hospital bed. I asked her what she thought. She said weeks. Maybe two. But she'd used the word weeks, not days. Not hours. Weeks. I let that roll around in my brain. Hypervigilance is exhausting.

From his hospice bed, he'd called out. The caregiver said she'd check on him. In the kitchen, I'd filled the droppers, made notes on the med chart in case whoever showed up that night was new. My father was to receive his morphine and Ativan through his feeding tube because he was refusing to take it orally. Night reports said he wasn't sleeping and told me to fill the syringes of Ativan to the max dosage for the night. I counted the vials, double-checked all the amounts were correct. When I'd left for the night as usual, he was dozing in his bed, and an hour after I was home, I got the call he'd collapsed in the hall bathroom.

Now hospice was telling me that they wouldn't take back the meds. I'd touched the meds. Handled the meds. Dosed the meds. Also, don't throw meds in the trash. Also, don't flush the meds. One trick is to use a chuck—an absorbent pad. Empty all the vials into the chuck, the hospice nurse told me, standing at the door, her bag slung over her shoulder. She wished me good luck. She told me again she was sorry. I promised I'd make sure she got paid for the day.

I pulled everything out of the fridge, all the vials I'd prepared. I pulled latex gloves on because you don't want the morphine touching your skin—God forbid you get any pain relief yourself—and started emptying the liquid into a chuck. One after another. Open, pour. Open, pour. The morphine would take away my cramps. Ativan for the crushing anxiety of this entire morning, week, month, life. My phone rang. He's dead, I had to tell them. His remaining friends he hadn't alienated. An old girlfriend. Dead, dead. Open, pour. Phone. Dead. The Ativan teased. Just a little, it said. Take the edge off. Pour, pour, pour. I poured the last one.

THE MURPHY BED

AFTER MY FATHER'S DEATH, I PRACTICED mindful giving. I took a single suit to the dry cleaners around the corner of my house, then a consignment shop downtown where I worked. Family members took his dishes and Keurig. I put a rusted Sears thermos from 1979 on eBay because it looked vintage and cool, and people like vintage and cool. Bags of clothing went to a local family shelter.

My husband and I organized a garage sale in his driveway. My daughter made piles of items she wanted that I had to talk her out of keeping: colorful ties, a large model sailboat, expired first aid kits. I told her she could keep any change she could find and gave her a small plastic bucket, which kept her occupied for hours searching through his couch and digging through his kitchen junk drawers. My father's neighbors poked through his belongings. The guy next door said my father used to walk around his backyard naked. A woman arrived in a small car. She gave me five dollars for my father's ancient, dusty vacuum. I offered to let people walk inside the house because we had a few pieces of furniture Habitat for Humanity hadn't taken. The retirement community's HOA patrol car showed up, said we needed a permit for an estate sale and, even then, an estate sale could not take place on the driveway. We piled the remainder of sellable items into my husband's truck and conducted a second garage sale at our house the following weekend. I relisted the thermos on eBay.

During the last weeks of my father's life when his siblings visited, they slept on the Murphy bed in the back room of my father's house. My husband and I could sell the Murphy bed. I took photographs. We folded it onto the wall, out of our way. I listed the bed on Craigslist for $200. Within the hour, I was flooded with messages. I set appointments for a Saturday, but when we arrived to my father's house that Saturday morning, we found the Murphy bed in pieces. We hadn't latched it correctly, we guessed. The sound of the bed coming off the wall and splintering must have been terrifying. I sent a text to the woman who I knew was on her way. I told her the truth. My father died. The Murphy bed fell off the wall and was now unsellable.

The woman said no problem. She was sorry about my dad. *Thank you for letting me know.* She said, *I'm not trying to be forward, but maybe your dad didn't want you to sell it.*

My father's ghost might have pushed the Murphy bed off the wall. I can't imagine he had a connection to the Murphy bed. He barely had a connection to his daughters.

Maybe!!!! I wrote to the woman. Too many exclamation points, but such were the times.

My husband and I hauled the pieces of the bed into the garage where the junk pile was growing. Making a junk pile inside a dead person's house felt immoral. You're providing a commentary on their life and their worth. This is garbage. This is not.

My father had commissioned my first husband to make a painting of a storefront he found interesting. The painting hung in my father's living room. My husband offhandedly said it'd look good in our guest room. I reminded him of the origin. *So?* he asked. If the painting had been from any of his exes, I would have suggested we burn it.

We sold my dad's car to a man who gave it to his teenage daughter. We sold his old truck to a guy who needed it for work. I hired a junk truck to scoop up the pile in the garage. I took the thermos off eBay.

Still, there was a small pile we took to our garage which contained, among other things: golf shoes, an ASU hat, two mismatched kitchen chairs, a table lamp, unstained potholders, two large stacks of pots and pans, a book: *Coach Wooden and Me*, a VCR, old maps of Phoenix, and a nightstand. We drove the nightstand to Goodwill. Each week, piece by piece, I threw items away until I finished the pile off in bulk trash. I kept the thermos, put it on my bookshelf, took it off my bookshelf, put it on the top shelf of my closet, took it off the top shelf of my closet, and walked it out to my trash can because I never wanted to keep it in the first place.

THE MAGIC ROOM

November 2019

A few weeks after my father's funeral, right before Thanksgiving, my mother called with news. "Grandma Sis fell again," she said. "It's bad this time."

Grandma Sis, my mother's mother, was eighty-nine. My mother was her only daughter. My sister and I her only grand-children. We lived in Arizona. She lived alone in the condo she'd lived in for forty-plus years in Illinois, where she'd lived most of her life. Her dementia advanced, yet she continued to pass her driving test. Every morning, she drove to get herself a coffee. She was not a frail old person. She was a cool old person. Extended family who lived nearby checked in on her, and that worked until it didn't.

The first time she fell in 2017, my mother and I made arrangements to go to her but Grandma Sis said no, she did not want my mother to come. After a month of conversation, she agreed it was okay for me, and only me, to visit. I left my young daughter and went to Illinois for four days. I took her to the doctor. I cleaned her condo, bought groceries. She was bruised up, bent over, easily tired. Yes, her short-term memory was questionable. Yes, one morning after I took her out for coffee and came back to her condo like usual, she sat at her dining room table, put her face in her hands, and sobbed because she'd forgotten we'd gone out for coffee. Yes, our nearby family members pulled me aside several times to tell me they believed she was not going to make it on her own and they were exhausted.

Also, she was fine. She was my Grandma Sis, and she was fine. While I was there, I wished I lived closer, or that she lived closer to me. I felt guilty leaving her. She stubbornly refused in-home help. No cleaners. No meal delivery. Without her knowledge, my mother hired a cleaning team who rang her condo bell one afternoon. Surprise! Your daughter hired us to help you! We're here to clean your condo. My grandmother invited them in for coffee cake, then told them to leave, they'd been hired by mistake. Grandma Sis was still charming and breezy and could work a room. She was a wounded animal putting on a show of strength because that was how she always survived.

Even before her that first fall, we'd tried to talk her into moving to Arizona. The conversation was never us moving back to Illinois, where she'd always lived. Her parents were buried in the cemetery in the middle of town. Her sister was in Chicago.

Now, the second major fall, and she had, somehow, lost her ability to walk. Like usual, that morning she'd walked to her car, driven to McDonald's, got her lattes, drove home.

She walked from her car to the elevator and collapsed. The doctors at the hospital could not provide an adequate explanation. The explanation for the ailment of every old person: old bodies are old bodies. "We can't do anything else for her in the hospital, but she needs constant care," the doctors said. She was malnourished and dehydrated. If she'd been alone in her condo, she might have been dead in twenty-four hours.

The hospital released her to a nursing home, where she did not sleep, did not eat, did not get up for exercises, and spent nights calling out to her own mother, who had been dead for twenty years.

Unable to walk, in pain, confused, but still, Grandma Sis told my mother not to come because she did not need her. Her condition deteriorated in the nursing home, and we were left with two options: she could move into assisted living in Illinois without close family near her, or move into assisted living in Arizona near my mom, sister, and me. I suggested we tell her she was coming to Arizona for a vacation. Assisted living was her worst nightmare, something she'd told me that under no terms would she accept. My mother finalized arrangements with a local facility. My mother would go to Illinois and bring Grandma Sis back.

When I was ten, my parents had moved our family out of Illinois in an effort to restart their marriage, and the idea of "home" provoked an identity crisis. Luckily, my sister and I went to Grandma Sis's, so safe and familiar, in the summer. She struggled with my sister's mood swings and impulsiveness, creating more tension between my mother and her, but she and I were close. In high school and college, I went alone to Grandma Sis's. I spent winter breaks from college with her. We drove into Chicago where we met up with my great-aunt and we saw plays and shopped at the big stores, things

I could not do in small-town Arizona. She took me to Italy. Later, when I had less time to travel, we spoke on the phone every week and made each other laugh.

My relationship with my father had been complicated, troubled, unhappy most of the time, and now, just weeks ago, his life had ended. Grandma Sis was not ending. She was injured. I argued with my mother: it should be me who went back to collect her.

"Why?" she asked.

"Well, you know, because I could probably make the transition for her a little smoother." We both knew. Grandma Sis responded better to me. My mother told me to stay home: my own daughter needed me.

She booked a flight. She'd go to Illinois the second week of December. In the mornings on my long commute to work, where I was trying to catch up and refocus after the chaos of my father's end-of-life care, I called Grandma Sis's room. Sometimes she answered, sometimes she didn't. Sometimes she was chipper, sometimes she moaned in pain. Each time I spoke with her, I said I'd see her soon and reminded her she was coming to Arizona for a vacation.

Often, I felt frustrated because I was not authorized to get updates from nursing home staff. Grandma Sis had made her cousin, one of the extended family members who lived locally, medical power of attorney. Her reason was, she'd said to my mother, the cousin *had not moved away*. My mother had.

"Punishing me, always," my mother said.

As Grandma Sis deteriorated and the decision was made to move her to Arizona, the cousin signed over power to my mother. My mother received the medical updates, which she filtered to me. Having gone through what I had with my father's final months, I was better equipped. I knew the language, the questions to ask. My superpower was calm in other people's crises. Whereas my mother was stressed, frantic at times. Angry. It should be me, I said over and over.

In the evenings, my daughter and I watched shows together, played dolls and hide-and-seek. "I Spy" for hours. One night, I asked her about her about my father, how she felt, if anything upset her (perhaps seeing a man cough and gasp for breath was scarring), but she shook her head, redirected me to the Disney Princess game we were playing.

"Who is your favorite princess?" she asked. "Grandma's favorite princess is Snow White."

Snow White slept in a glass box in the forest waiting for a man to come save her. I told my daughter my favorite princesses were Elsa. Moana. The fighters.

I called my mother to ask why she was telling my daughter Snow White was her favorite princess. Snow White needed to be saved. She could not save herself. Not the best message.

"Snow White was banished to the forest by the Evil Queen because she was never accepted, but she came out all right in end," my mother said and didn't want to discuss it further.

I was on my lunchbreak, sitting in my counselor's office. I did not know which direction to go: Grandma Sis or my father. It felt strange to feel happy that my grandmother was coming, even though under sad circumstances, but maybe that was the child in me. I felt despair and hopelessness because my alcoholic father who'd been gone for most of my life was now gone forever, but that was also the child in me.

"Where do you feel all that in your body?" she asked.

The body question was one of her favorites. She asked me all the time. And all the time, I did not know the answer. I felt it everywhere. Nowhere.

"Here," I said and put my hand over my heart. That felt close to right.

"No," she replied. "Where do you feel it in your body?"

I kept my hand over my heart. I put another hand around the back of my neck.

"I don't know," I said.

We sat in silence. She waited for me to give her a real answer.

Stiff neck. I'd slept on the couch. The night before, my husband and I'd had an argument. He went upstairs, and I stayed downstairs. I watched *Coco*, the Pixar movie based on the Mexican tradition of Día de los Muertos, the one night of the year when ancestors can come back to the Land of the Living. The movie is fun and cute until the end when it's devastating. I'd seen it for the first time after my cousin died, and now I watched it when I needed to cry. In the movie, the boy, Miguel, wants to play music against his family's wishes, and he is transported into the Land of the Dead, where he meets his ancestors, including his great-great-grandfather, who was a musician but banished from the family. Part of the movie is about a man Miguel meets trying to get back to his living daughter, who was a toddler when he died but is now at the end of her life with a failing memory. The girl is Miguel's grandmother. A father who left. A grandmother who lost her memory. Reconciliation. Gutting.

The argument was about my husband wanting to go out with some guys over the weekend. We'd had my father's funeral luncheon in our backyard and the chairs were still outside, getting dirty, and coolers on the patio were still full of melted ice and cans of beer. The coolers needed to be dumped. Was that beer good anymore? I'd bought Old Milwaukee, the beer my dad drank when I was a kid. My alcoholic father died, and I put out his favorite beer during my childhood, like an enabler. When I lived in my father's house after my divorce from my first husband, he'd come home in the evening with a case—a case—of Miller Light and a bag of Kit Kats. I often found Kit Kat wrappers on his counter and a recycling bin full of empty bottles. The Miller Light might have gone over better.

Someone needed to dump the water in the coolers, and my husband wanted to go out. I wanted to know why I was the one who had to dump the water. I had to write thank-you notes, and I didn't know where we should keep my father's urn. Who else was going to write the thank-you notes? No one.

My husband was unclear about why I was upset. He'd cleaned the yard before the luncheon. Fixed the horseshoe pit. Trimmed the trees. He made large, sweeping gestures. My father was dead. It was all over. He did not understand. Once grief comes in, it doesn't go back out. It shifts, changes shape. It gets lighter or heavier. But it's always there in some form.

I screamed he was abandoning me. I sobbed and yelled and stomped my feet and sat on the floor of our living room and crossed my arms. "You don't get it, you can't get it," I yelled at him. "Fucking go out then."

I hit play on *Coco*, cried into the pillow so hard I had broken blood vessels under my eyes.

December 2019

Holding two McDonald's bags, I waited outside The Meadows, my grandmother's new home, with my daughter and sister. Grandma Sis's Welcoming Committee. My daughter eyed the bags because she knew there were french fries inside. I had one bag for my mother, another for Grandma Sis. What you give to one, you must give to the other. The airport shuttle arrived. My mother hopped out of the back. Grandma Sis was in the passenger front seat. The driver removed the wheelchair and luggage and Grandma Sis. He said to her, "Take care of yourself, Mama. Be good now."

My daughter tapped my arm and asked for a french fry. "One second, OK?" I said for the fifth time.

My mother pushed the wheelchair toward me. Until that moment, Grandma Sis on her way, I'd imagined us going out for coffee together, going to the mall. I'd convinced myself of my own lie: she was on vacation.

Inside the wheelchair sat a bruised woman in a shoulder sling. This woman was not my grandmother. My grandmother was spry, quick, put together. My mother's father died from a heart attack in 1959 when my mother was nine, and Grandma Sis had gone into the workforce when women were supposed to "be home." She'd worked in a high-rise in Chicago. She never walked—she power walked. Now, she was confused about how to move in the chair. I bent to hug her. She used her good hand to pat my arm.

"That man thought I was his mother," she said of the driver. She waved to him. "That was a terrible ride."

My daughter tapped on my arm again. She wanted those french fries. I put the McDonald's bag in Grandma Sis's lap.

She removed the burger, took two small bites, the way a child might do when they believe an adult is tricking them into trying new food. My mother, tight-lipped and tense, accepted her McDonald's bag with a nod.

"How did it go?" I asked, vague on purpose.

"Fine until the meds started to wear off," my mother said. "And then—"

I held up my hand. My boundary. The one I'd invited my mother to break. I kept my family members in boxes in my head—even in my thoughts, I needed them to be separate from each other. My mother's sense of duty and mine were not the same.

Clutching the McDonald's bag, my mother said she had to check in at the front desk to get my grandmother in her room. The Meadows, like most assisted living facilities, was divided three ways. The independent living side could come and go as they pleased. They lived in apartments and drove cars and went out at night. The middle section had call buttons in their rooms for extra help, but most residents were mobile. The third section, where Grandma Sis would live, was Memory Care. A group of hip, happy seniors walked out of The Meadows in the direction of a van waiting to take them to the casino. I waved to them, like, See? Friends! My grandmother didn't gamble. She stuck out her lower lip and pouted.

"Why are there so many old people here?" she asked. "Am I in Arizona?"

I put my finger over my lips. "Shhh. We don't want to offend anyone." She took another bite of her burger, swallowed. My daughter again tapped my arm. She asked me to bend down and whispered in my ear she wanted to know when she could have a french fry. Grandma Sis gave the building in front of her a once-over. She saw the cactus, the rocks, the desert landscaping.

"Am I in Arizona?" she asked again.

I explained, like I'd done on the phone before she arrived, like my mother had done when she walked into her room at the nursing home in Illinois: You got in your car—you weren't supposed to be driving, by the way. You drove across the street to your favorite place, McDonald's. You got your lattes. One for the morning. One to heat up later. You collapsed in the garage of your condo building after. Your neighbor called 911. You went to the hospital where they called Mom and told her it appeared you hadn't drunk any water in three days. How is that possible? Surely you were at least drinking water because if you don't drink water, you will die and everyone knows this. Anyway, this will be great fun. I'm ten miles away instead of 2,000. You're here! And we're here! Your daughter, your granddaughters, your great-granddaughter. Your family is here to take care of you.

My daughter tugged on my arm, pointed to the french fries.

"No, no," I said, annoyance rising. "These are for Grandma Sis. Grandma Sis needs to eat."

"Oh, let her have them," Grandma Sis said. "It's all right. Do you want the french fries?"

My daughter lit up.

"Give her the french fries," she said as though withholding them from my daughter was a tragedy.

She gave the bag to my daughter. My daughter's toddler hand—tiny, smooth—contrasted against my grandmother's—paper-thin skin bruised purple from IVs.

"Am I in Arizona?" my grandmother asked again.

"Yes. Your vacation," I said. I opened a water bottle and made her drink some, most of which spilled on her shirt.

January 2020

Staff buzzed my daughter and I into Memory Care. Grandma Sis was not in her room. We checked the dining area. Twelve wheelchairs, my daughter counted out loud, proud of herself. Grandma Sis was not in the TV area. We returned to the dining room. My daughter spotted her first. I, again, did not recognize her. In the five weeks she'd been at The Meadows, she'd refused help bathing. Her hair was slick with grease. She was wearing someone else's shirt.

We passed a staff member chatting with two residents. "Your name is Henry, and his name is George," she said to the man. "You two are friends."

George was upset and insisted he was not friends with Henry while Henry sat back, shook his head, like everything was ridiculous.

The staff member smiled at my daughter, gave me a little eye roll and smiled. My mother thought it was wrong to bring my daughter to visit. Everyone moaning, my mother said. Scary for little kids. I said it was important my daughter spend time with Grandma Sis for as long as she could. I said that, anyway, it wasn't a bad thing to expose her to the end of life. Grandma Sis used to take me on the rounds. Elderly relatives curled up in bed, dying in their homes. At my great-grandmother's nursing home twenty years ago, a man screamed and cursed all day and all night. Grandma Sis rolled her eyes at him, sighed loudly. It all ends, often in the most miserable way.

Joan and Nancy

Cousins of my grandmother, thrice removed, some chain like that, Joan and Nancy were sisters. They lived in the house they'd grown up in, a few blocks from my grandma's condo, and we visited them.

In my childhood, Joan and Nancy were always old. Joan had wispy white hair, lots of dark chin hair, and weeded her front yard from morning to night even as her hands shook. She was never not in her front yard in her apron picking weeds when Grandma and I pulled up in the drive. Joan took us inside to her living room, a relic of 1950. Three large portraits of children hung on the wall: Joan, Nancy, and Leo, their brother, now long gone, dead. We had a routine. We sat on the plastic-covered furniture and Joan offered us pizzelles. That was her thing. She made pizzelles, hundreds of them. My grandma always held her car keys to show we intended to stay only a few minutes. We intended to be polite, we were doing our duty. Joan signaled it was time to see Nancy. She led us down the hall, opened the bedroom door. There was Nancy in her hospital bed, curled into a fetal position, moaning. She was in advanced Alzheimer's. Joan cared for her most of the time, but a nurse came in a few hours a day for relief. Nancy always had a fresh bow in her hair. Someone came in and brushed and washed Nancy's hair once a week, put a bow in it. Joan always said, "Isn't she beautiful?"

"Oh yes," my grandma said. "Beautiful."

Grandma Sis shuffled me out the door and we sat in the front seats of her car. She always thanked me for going with her as though the choice had been mine. The first time I'd met the sisters, I'd pulled the visor down to look in the mirror at my chin, wondering if I also had chin hair in my future, and if I did, would I let it get away from me the way Joan had.

Grandma said, "Joan has to let Nancy go. That's the problem. She won't let Nancy go."

Nancy and Joan had a nice house. Brick. Solid. Clean inside. Their father had been an overbearing man, Grandma told me. Nancy had met someone, a long time ago, but their father wouldn't allow her to get married. He wouldn't allow her to leave. He let the brother go, but not the sisters.

"Why?" I'd asked.

Grandma Sis started her car, turned the AM radio up. "I don't know. I never asked. But they were born in that house and they'll die in that house. Don't ever put a bow in my hair."

After Nancy finally passed on and Joan went downhill, my grandmother was named executor of their estate. She had worked for the IRS. Everyone went to her for estate questions, tax questions, financial questions. Everyone trusted her.

At the dining room table, Grandma Sis clutched my arm. "You're here to take me home, right?"

Home to her condo. Home was not The Meadows, being wheeled in for lunch.

I linked my arm through hers. "How about you let them help you shower?" I asked. "You'll feel better. That's how you will heal."

Grandma Sis made a face. My daughter sat at the table next to me, staring at the other people. One woman moaned and my daughter zeroed in on her. I shook my head. We don't stare at people. My daughter opened her eyes wide and raised her eyebrows, which I knew meant a sarcastic, in a four-year-old way, *Sorry*. Maybe my mother was right. Having her here was too much.

A woman at my grandmother's table asked a staff member for dessert. The staff member reminded the woman she was diabetic. "Rats," the woman said to us.

Grandma Sis asked about my mother. She was here yesterday, I said. My grandma took a bite of her pumpkin pie. The woman asking for dessert eyed the pie.

Grandma Sis asked again about my mom. I said my mom was at her own home, but she'd been here yesterday. Grandma put her fork down. She had pumpkin pie on her mouth, so I picked up a napkin and wiped it off. She asked, when was my mother coming? When was my mother calling a cab for her to take her to the airport? Grandma Sis had capacity. I understood she knew who she was, who we were. She knew she was in a place she'd never wanted to be in.

I explained my mother wouldn't come back today. Maybe tomorrow. Maybe in a few days. I shifted the conversation to what they'd served for lunch.

"Pork and beans," she said.

"Like you're on a camping trip?" I laughed at my own joke.

She announced she was finished, though she'd barely eaten the pie. I encouraged her to drink more water, but she refused. I wheeled her to her room. My daughter wanted to help, so she held one handle of the wheelchair, and I held the other, and together we pushed Grandma Sis down the hall. For a moment, the three of us moved like a unified front. No complaints. No tears. We walked in sync, all of us with one goal: get Grandma Sis to her room.

Her neighbor, the woman who lived in the room across the hall, could walk. We passed her, and Grandma Sis turned and looked up at me. "That woman is a mean woman," she said, but I didn't ask how, I didn't want to know, and I figured, also, Grandma Sis didn't know. Grandma Sis said, "When is your mother coming?"

I was tired. I didn't answer. I opened the door to her room and pushed her inside. The Meadows was a newer facility. The floors were shining hardwood. She had her own bathroom, a living room area, and a bedroom area. Her room was bigger and nicer than my first apartment. Family provided the furniture. My mother had made a trip to a furniture store and purchased a loveseat, a TV, a TV stand, a coffee table that held pictures, and a small end table that was collecting unused cans of Ensure, plastic bags, empty McDonald's coffee cups, and boxes of tissue.

I wheeled her next to the loveseat, helped her stand. She was off balance, nervous, like a child learning to walk. I asked if she was in pain, if her hips hurt. No, she said. Yes, she said. I helped her pivot and sit. She winced and clutched her shoulder, still in a sling. I placed a pillow under her feet on the ottoman and noticed her pant legs were soaking wet.

"Did you spill something?" I asked.

My father's legs had swelled up and leaked fluid, but he he'd been dying from cancer. My grandmother was not dying. She was recovering from a fall. I peeled back her pant legs to see her swollen ankles. I washed my hands.

Grief was my new year's resolution.

Grandma Sis asked why her shoulder hurt. Instead of explaining, I asked if she wanted to talk to her sister, who had an iPhone. We could FaceTime. They could see each other. My daughter interrupted. She brought over pictures from the other side of the room and asked my grandma to identify the people in them. She and I did this together at home. My grandmother's parents. My daughter held my wedding photo and pointed to me, my husband, then my grandmother. She pointed to my father. A light clicked on: Grandma Sis asked how my father was doing. I reminded her he'd died three months earlier.

She shook her fist in frustration at herself. "I knew it," she said. "I'm sorry." Then, "Who's handling his estate?"

"Me," I said. "Oh, remember what a mess it was after Joan and Nancy died?"

Grandma Sis looked blank.

"Do you remember how their nurse somehow got Joan to sign over the house to her and moved in after Joan died? That was a mess, wasn't it?"

My father's estate was straightforward, but still, I'd never handled one. I'd never shut down a person's life. Junk mail in his name was coming to my house. We still had not completed emptying out his house. My husband and I worked full-time, and now Grandma Sis was here. The person I needed to help me sat in front of me needing my help.

"I outlived your father," Grandma Sis said.

"You did," I agreed.

She nodded, satisfied. "Your father was a handsome man," she said. "That was his undoing."

She remembered how much she hated my father, so this was a good sign. I glanced at her soaking wet ankles.

Suddenly, she said she had to go to the bathroom. I looked for a caregiver but could not find one. No time. My grandma and my mom both were fond of telling me that when I was a kid, I refused to let anyone but the two of them take me to the bathroom. Now, I pushed my grandma in her wheelchair to use the toilet. She was not a big person, but she was confused, and she was deadweight.

"We are both going to give our all on the count of three for you to get up from the chair and pivot to the toilet," I said.

She reached for the handicap bar, and I put my arm under hers. She stood, struggling with her pants, the musty smell of her body overwhelming. I helped her pull down her pants and underwear. A tingling rushed through my chest. My body tensed. She was a fall risk. But I couldn't stay. She needed dignity. The bathroom door was a sliding door, and I stood with my back to her on the other side.

"I don't need this handicap bar," my grandma said.

"I know," I said, and fought the urge to cry.

A caregiver came into the room for a check, and I said my grandmother needed help in the bathroom. I tidied the end table. My daughter rearranged the pictures on the coffee table. "I want to go home, Mom," she said. I nodded. I could do that.

Grandma Sis fell again. Again. The caregivers placed mats next to her bed. With each fall, she grew more insistent she was fine on her own. She argued with everyone that she didn't belong in assisted living. She called my mother four times an hour asking her to call a cab and buy a plane ticket. She called her sister in Chicago, who was also not doing well, so frequently and causing her so much agitation that my mother made the decision to remove the phone from her room. I remembered Grandma Sis telling me about a friend of hers who'd died a few years earlier, whose children put her in a nursing home and had to remove her phone because she called 911 every day to report she'd been kidnapped. Grandma Sis had shaken her head. "Can you believe that?" she'd said.

The next fall, she was taken to the hospital.

My mother sent me a text message during work to ask if it was a good time to talk. It was not a good time to talk. I worked hard to compartmentalize all the swirling crises: mornings were for my daughter, lunch breaks were for counseling or for phone calls or errands involving my father's estate, evenings were for visiting Grandma Sis. That day, I had counseling. I didn't want to deal with anything other than reconciling my father's death, my aloneness in my grief about him. I texted *If it's not an emergency we can talk later*, but she called anyway.

"The doctors at the hospital think Grandma Sis should go into hospice," she said.

I was stunned. That weekend, I'd brought Grandma Sis her McDonald's coffee latte and she'd thanked me. Obviously, she did not need hospice. I held my phone to my ear while I walked to my car.

I blurted the only thing I could think of. "Does Grandma want to go into hospice?"

My father had chosen hospice. He'd said the words out loud to me. I could not imagine Grandma Sis saying anything like that.

"Hospice will bring in a bed with guardrails," my mother said.

She started to explain, but I cut her off. "I fucking know how hospice works. I managed Dad's hospice."

I was driving, making angry turns and watching the road get blurry. I used my thumb to wipe away tears. Always a good time to fall apart before you even walk through your therapist's door.

My mother continued. "The doctors at the hospital told me they think she'll forget who we are soon."

"I don't believe that. I don't think that will happen."

My mother sighed.

"I have to go."

I pulled into my counselor's parking lot and stared out the windshield, then snatched my bag off the passenger seat and stormed into her office on fire. The doctors were wrong. Grandma Sis needed to go home to her condo. I'd take her. I'd get tickets, get her on a plane, and take her home. I wanted to give her what she wanted like I'd tried to do for my father. That's what you're supposed to do. Complicated or not.

I started to cry. I couldn't stop. Twenty-two years of on-and-off counseling without welling up. Now I was sobbing, like a child.

My father was not a good father. He existed in the role and nothing more, and then his bad choices killed him. I'd spent my life angry at him. Then I accepted that he was who he was and I couldn't change it. The end. Then he died because that's what people do. They die. It wasn't, it would never be, *My most loving and supportive person in my life* is gone.

Grief wasn't only what you lost but also what you never had. In snatches of spare time, I'd started to write about him in a way I couldn't when he'd been alive, all the things I could never say: alcoholism, regrets, that goddamn dress story turning into a sad story not a joke, arguments. I wanted to make something out of the relationship I'd had with him. Give it meaning. My relationship with Grandma Sis had meaning. My dad was a person. My grandma was *my* person. The person I went to. Had gone to. I was hysterical. My counselor suggested we try a breathing exercise.

I placed my hands on my stomach. Breathe in. Breathe out. I went back: I was young, maybe seven or eight. In our old house in Illinois. It was winter, dark and cold, early morning.

No talk about moving yet. Woods surrounded our house. My sister and I built forts. We had friends in the neighborhood and at school. I walked downstairs through the living room and stood in the entryway to the kitchen. My mother sat on the floor in her faded yellow robe next to a heating vent, smoking a cigarette. The ashtray was near her feet. She said she was getting warm. My father wasn't home, but he should have been. It was just us: my mom, my sister, and me.

This was the sadness I couldn't say out loud. My father was not home because he was never home. My mother sat alone because she thought she deserved it, thought someday a switch might come on in his head and he'd stop all his bullshit carousing and boozing and return, fully present, to his family. My sister was upstairs, asleep, oblivious to it all. And there I was, in that entryway, watching her watch the door, holding the weight of both of their choices, though I was too young to understand that then.

The exercise was over. My hour was up. On my way back to work, I called my mother and briskly told her hospice would ask for a funeral home to keep on file. I used Waverly Brothers for Dad. They were great. I hung up.

March 2020

I sat outside The Meadows waiting for my temperature check and screening questions. A resident from the independent living side sat next to me. She'd been out at the casino. Her white hair was curled and fluffed to the moon. She tapped her cane on the concrete between her legs like nervous people shake a foot. She told everyone who passed by she didn't want to go back in because they'd taken all the salt and pepper shakers off the tables.

"There's no virus." She pointed her cane at the front doors. "There's only tyranny."

I had masks on backorder. Friends who taught in higher ed had already been sent home. My daughter's preschool hadn't been scheduled to reopen until after spring break.

"This is all to get Joe Biden elected," she practically spat.

A staff member in full PPE standing outside the front doors motioned it was my turn, so I jumped up and walked in the front entryway.

My temperature read 99.4.

My heart started to beat fast. I put my hands to my cheeks. This is it. I have it. I nearly turned back to that woman. Do you see now? It's in me. It's happening. I took shallow breaths, feeling everything sway under me. I placed my hand on the folding table to steady myself, the list of names and temperatures nearby. The woman shook the thermometer, said that had been happening all day. People stood out in the sun and got hot foreheads. She suggested I move into the shade for ten minutes then she'd take it again. I walked around to the side of the building and leaned against the hot brick, trying to calm myself.

By my second round, after I'd cooled down, my temperature had dropped and I was allowed in. I washed my hands in the first bathroom on the way to the memory care unit. Already, my knuckles were red, cracked, and bleeding from washing so much. Staff had given the code to get into the unit since I was there so often and I buzzed myself in, but because I'd touched the code box, I washed my hands again in the next bathroom. A dispenser on the wall held latex gloves. I stared at them, disbelieving. I'd searched high and low for latex gloves but no one had them in stock. Before I could talk myself out of it, before I could reason that gloves were more important in this facility than for me in the grocery store, I stuffed four into a zippered pocket in my bag.

I found my grandma asleep in the TV room, covered in a black velour blanket printed with yellow stars that did not belong to her. Several residents in wheelchairs watched the movie on TV. One man on the couch opposite my grandma snored lightly, his mouth open.

Grandma Sis opened her eyes. A tiny woman, a resident more mobile than the others, flitted through the room, touched each person on their shoulder and told them she loved them. She stopped in front of Grandma Sis and told her she loved her. Grandma Sis came alive for a moment, and said she loved her as well. This brought me immense joy. Maybe my grandma had made a friend. She wasn't suffering alone.

"Who is that?" I asked.

"I don't know," she said.

She asked me to take her to her room, so I started to get her ready, but staff stopped me. She had to stay in the main front area because she fell so much and they didn't have enough people on hand to check on her every five minutes. I directed her attention to the TV. Grandma Sis shook her head the way my daughter did when she was mad at me. Grandma Sis became agitated and tried to get up. This was something I noticed among all residents: for a period of time, it was hard to tell if they were asleep or zoned out, then suddenly they became animated and grasped the handles of the wheelchair as if to stand. I watched one woman rock herself all the way out of the chair and take a wobbly step forward before a staff member rushed toward her and the woman collapsed in the staff member's arms.

"Does my mother know where I am?" Grandma Sis asked.

My mother. Not your mother. My mother said she'd told Grandma Sis she was in hospice, but insisted she would forget because she didn't have any short-term memory. When my father was dying, he had delusions, and he forgot. I'd once sat with him for an hour explaining everything to him: you have cancer, you chose hospice, you are dying. Grandma Sis didn't remember where she was, but I could tell her. I could walk her through everything. Instead, I answered her: "Yes. She knows."

I tried to level my breathing, afraid I was on the edge of another panic attack. The room swayed. What if I was having a stroke? I touched my face. No, now I had to wash my hands again, find sanitizer and rub it on the spot where my fingers had touched my cheek. My throat was dry—the virus.

Covid wanted the nursing homes. People like me transported it inside. As I sat in the TV room, among this group of vulnerable people, all of them at end of their life, all of them unaware of what was going on outside, I knew I had to leave. I covered my mouth. The virus was airborne. The virus was not airborne. News said it was airborne. News said it wasn't airborne. The CDC said masks are best but stopped short of saying airborne. I stood, hugged my grandma, turning my face away from her, pulled the blanket over her and told her I'd be back soon. She closed her eyes, touched the blanket, murmured it was her mother's blanket, her mother had sewed it for her and wasn't it beautiful? I held her hand lightly. She was so fragile, I was afraid if I put too much pressure in the squeeze she might break. I said I'd see her soon, but I never saw Grandma Sis in person again.

Michelle

I used the code to buzz myself out of the memory care unit and passed Michelle, the staff person who was my favorite. She smiled, said she hadn't seen my mother recently. I smiled too, said maybe my mother would come later today though I knew that wasn't true. My mother didn't want to come at all. Now with Covid, she had a reason.

Michelle was a tall Black woman. Young. Most of the staff who worked at The Meadows were Black.

"I was going to check on your grandma," she said.

"She's sleeping. She doesn't seem well. Confused."

Michelle nodded. "She's been more confused lately."

I held my hands in front of me like I was going into surgery. I needed to wash them again.

The following day, The Meadows closed to visitors. They sent all residents to their rooms. There was no testing and limited PPE. For their safety, the dementia patients, the Alzheimer's patients all sat alone in their rooms, no stimulation, no social interaction. All isolated from each other, themselves, and their families.

April 2020

I drove past The Meadows on my way to pick up cleaning supplies stored at my father's house. The chemo had knocked out his immune system, and he'd had a thriving case of thrush when he died. I'd bought vats of bleach and Lysol wipes. Past Me, but always Hypochondriac Me, had unknowingly stockpiled for a pandemic.

Someone had taped red paper hearts on all the lower windows of The Meadows. Big signs dotted the front: Heroes work here. Grandma Sis's room was on the corner. I could tap on the window. We could talk.

No. What if I had the virus and she breathed it in through the screen? What if she had the virus and I breathed it in through the screen? They—the CDC, the governor, friends on social media, the actual media—all said sorry, you can't see your grandparents. They all said, do you want your grandparents to die? Conduct your life as though you have the virus—extra helpful for those of us who suffer from extreme health anxiety. Every breath you exhale is a chance for the virus to settle into the vulnerable. I stayed home. I wore a mask if I had to go out. I stopped making eye contact with people. They all said, but the essential workers need to stay. Michelle, everyone who worked in The Meadows, they all needed to continue to go to work and risk their lives to take care of other people's family members.

I made angry phone calls to the Arizona governor. I sent angry emails to the Arizona state legislature. We need more tests. We need more PPE. Look at South Korea! South Korea is nailing it. Never mind, the bars were in crisis. The governor needed to open the bars for the economy. Let's do it for the economy. The bars had to bring in the money and the people needed to drink.

Inexplicably, my grandmother regained her ability to walk. She woke up one morning, got out of bed, walked out of her room, into the hall, and opened the back door to The Meadows, setting off all the alarms. She wanted a cab to the airport. Terminal patients have a burst of energy. They regain control of their dying bodies for a day, two days. Then the rally is over. Young people wanted to go out and drink, and please for the love of capitalism, let them go. Hospice gave my grandmother Ativan to temper her agitation. I told my mother that if anything, Grandma Sis saying she wanted to go home was a good thing.

Michelle and I backchanneled. She let Grandma Sis use her phone so we could FaceTime, but all Grandma Sis wanted to do was talk about getting a cab, getting on a plane, and going home. Terminal patients talk about going home or going on a trip. They want to leave their shoes by the door, have their wallet and keys ready. But this was not true for *my* grandma because she knew she wasn't home. This was not a dying person and that doctor at the hospital was wrong. She knew who we all were, and she knew who she was. This woman needed to make plans.

For seven weeks, I called as often as I could, though I had to time it for when Michelle was working. We chatted a bit the first few times, but Grandma Sis grew more confused, more agitated. Soon after, when I called, Michelle told me Grandma Sis was sleeping. I asked if she shouldn't be eating now. But no, Grandma Sis wanted to sleep. She wanted to be in bed, asleep, and not wake up for anything.

May 2020

My mother, sister, and I stood outside The Meadows in front of Grandma Sis's room. At my insistence. It was May but already over a hundred degrees. The bush in front of us was filled with bees. Hospice reported to my mother Grandma Sis was not getting out of bed. I already knew this from Michelle. Grandma Sis slept twenty-three hours a day and refused all food and water.

Restaurants and businesses were open again, but The Meadows restricted all visitors. Staff told my mother they'd grant an exception for us to come in through a back door and say goodbye. Two weeks earlier, a staff member had tested positive and so all residents and staff were tested. Grandma Sis was negative, but it had taken eleven days for results. We had cloth masks but that was all. I was working from home, consuming mass amounts of news. I read every single Covid death story I could find, my anxiety spiral peaking each day before lunch. A young man, younger than me, in his 30s, who'd sat next to his father's bedside as his father died from Covid, got and died from Covid.

My mother, sister, and I agreed we could not go inside The Meadows. My mother was vulnerable because of her age. My sister was vulnerable because of her various health conditions. It was unclear what Covid did to young children like my daughter. Still, I insisted we find a way to say goodbye to Grandma Sis. My idea was to talk to her through her window on the first floor, but the problem was that Grandma Sis was in bed.

My sister already wanted to go. Too many bees.

A staff member—a white woman I'd never seen before—who maybe didn't know, or who maybe was tired, or who maybe had a casual attitude about the whole thing, tried to wake my dying grandmother and coax her into her wheelchair. My grandmother came to slightly, allowed herself to be put in the chair. The staff member wheeled her to the window. My grandma's head rolled to one side. Back to sleep. Once she saw us, she'd be active and chatty, I'd thought. She'd come to, realize her family was there. Realize I was. The staff member patted her cheek, pointed to us.

My mother's hand covered her mouth in shock. She hadn't seen Grandma Sis since March.

"She's so small," my mother said.

Grandma Sis barely filled the wheelchair. The staff member picked up my grandma's hand and waved at us. That was it. I was done. This was a folly.

"Put her back," I said through the bees, through the window. "We're done. Put her back in bed." We backed away while the staff member waved my grandma's hand.

My mother arranged for Last Rites. A few days later, Grandma Sis died alone in her room.

Michelle texted me. She was in the room with Grandma Sis earlier in the day before she died. She'd held her hand, told her we were all with her and named our names. Grandma Sis squeezed her hand back. I didn't know if that was true or not, but it was comforting, and I appreciated Michelle telling me.

June 2020

I wanted to be there when they took my grandmother out of The Meadows. A woman in scrubs walked toward me in the parking lot. The hospice nurse. She wore a cloth mask. I wore a cloth mask. We stood in the bright, hot June sun. Sweat was pooling under my hair and I knew soon it would run down my back.

"I've been talking to your mom on the phone," the hospice nurse said.

"I know," I said. "She isn't coming. It's only me."

The Waverly Brothers van backed into the parking space near us. A Waverly—only one this time—stepped out.

"You picked up my dad," I blurted.

He asked me my father's name. I told him, and he said he remembered. I told him both he and his brother had come that day. He said they like to go together, but they'd been so busy lately.

He, the hospice nurse, and I all stood six feet apart in a strange circle.

The Waverly disappeared inside and returned with my grandmother on the gurney, a sheet covering her face. He asked if I wanted to see her. No. I wanted to make sure she wasn't alone when she came out. That was all. Tears and sweat soaked my mask. The hospice nurse made like she was going to hug me but stopped herself. No touching. I was alone, again, watching my grandma's body get loaded into the van.

In my car, I watched the Waverly Brothers van drive away. I texted work, told them I wasn't coming in for a few days, at least two. My father had died six months earlier and now, sorry, more death. More missed days of work. I'd be back on Monday. I drove home, past the McDonald's I'd taken to stopping at when I'd visited her. The McDonald's I hadn't been to since the start of the pandemic.

At home, numb, I poured a glass of wine. First, my habit now, I sniffed inside the glass to make sure I still had a sense of smell. I pulled up old voicemails from Grandma Sis, wondered how I'd known two years ago to start saving every message she left. I wondered how I'd been in denial for so long about her decline when all anyone had to do was listen to her voice.

———————

I wrote Grandma Sis's obituary. I sent Michelle a copy of it:

Widowed at age 29, Sis took off her apron, a garment that never suited her, and entered the workforce to support her nine-year-old daughter. She secured a job with the federal government, working her way up from typist to accountant to district manager of the Chicago division of the Internal Revenue Service—never did she abbreviate to IRS—often the lone woman both in management and company photos. Tax season was her Christmas. She studied tax law changes the way some people read gossip magazines. Well into her 80s, she was the go-to tax preparer for family, friends, neighbors, and priests. Somehow, she pushed through her pathologic aversion to any restroom that was not her own and, upon retirement, traveled the world with her sister, notably to Italy, Egypt, Greece, and Turkey. She was never without coffee cake for a guest and never without stories of the old days: the big Italian family dinners, the work her parents did during WWII, or a difficult audit she completed during her working years. She was also never without bleach, germ averse long before it was trending. Sis loved Macy's, control, and McDonald's "coffee lattes."

Michelle responded with a video, one she'd taken of Grandma Sis in the weeks leading up to her death, during her brief moment of the mock recovery when she'd regained her ability to walk and tried to escape. A weak, flickering version of Grandma Sis stood in the hall outside her room, one hand on the railing for support, the other on her hip, her head down, panting, wincing. Michelle encouraged her to keep walking.

"Come on," Michelle said. "You can do this. You're almost there. You're a strong woman."

"No," Grandma Sis replied. Her voice was broken. "No, no, no, no."

I watched the video two times through, thanked Michelle for sending it, wished her well, hoped she was staying as safe as possible. The video stayed in my phone for a day, maybe two. I couldn't watch it again, couldn't be reminded of what I missed, what I failed to do, how I'd broken my vow and left her alone. Delete.

My mother dropped seven large black garbage bags at my house. The Meadows had bagged Grandma Sis's belongings, and my mother didn't want them. I offered to do the sorting, though I didn't remember Grandma going in with that much stuff.

The bags sat unopened in my garage for three weeks like unstable dynamite. Who had touched the outside of the bags? The objects inside? Whose breath full of Covid was trapped inside that plastic? I let the bags simmer in the hot garage, hoping the Arizona summer heat would kill whatever was inside. I treated her belongings like a disease, after I'd left her alone to die, and all of it made me sick, ate me up inside.

The Magic Room

When I stayed with Grandma Sis during high school, college, and beyond, we had a routine. She quietly opened the door to my bedroom in the early morning to fetch my laundry. She was up at 4 a.m. everyday drinking coffee, picking up her paper, reading the obituaries and the stocks, taking down the trash, after cleaning the clean kitchen and dusting the dust-free coffee table, and chatting with other neighbors also up at 4 a.m. picking up their papers and taking out their trash. She tiptoed into my room and swept all my dirty clothes into her arms so she could wash, dry, and iron them before I woke. Her anxiety was loud and unstoppable, and cleaning and doing obsessive amounts of laundry was her antianxiety medicine. When I woke, she had a second pot of (weak) coffee ready for me and she walked me through my laundered clothes, showing me what stage of drying a certain article was in or how she'd ironed a shirt. She paced outside the kitchen waiting for me to finish my toast so she could unplug the machine and tuck it back under the counter. When she sensed I was finished with my coffee, she'd swoop in and whisk the cup off the table. She needed tasks. I needed to be cared for. I called the guest room where I slept The Magic Room because I'd go to bed surrounded by dirty laundry and wake up with all my clothes washed. She laughed at this no matter how many times I said it.

It was well into July, almost a full month after she died, when I opened The Meadows bags. The first was full of blankets. None of them hers. Another was full of pants and shirts, all sized extra-large, some labeled with other people's names. I unfolded a pair of extra-small, bright-purple stretch pants. The right size, but she would never have worn them. Five bags in, I found her purse, a midlevel brand utility bag. Signature Grandma Sis purse: not expensive but not cheap, functional, and beige. Inside the purse, I found loose change, a brown and gold lipstick holder with a green-capped, orange-red lipstick inside. The lipstick had melted. In a front pocket, I found thirty-five dollars. I shoved all the clothing that wasn't hers back into the bags and piled them in the corner.

The clothing I'd recognized as hers, I would wash, fold, and arrange as neatly as possible like those that had appeared in The Magic Room all those mornings in the past.

ALL SOULS

IN 2021, WE'RE IN A parade. A celebration. Thousands of us. A community. We're walking in the All Souls Procession for Día de los Muertos in Tucson. We're mourning, but we're mourning with drums and fiddles and dancing and sugar skulls and big, bright dresses. The noise, for a moment, cancels out the grief, fills in the silent space.

It feels good to be with people. I don't like people, but this pandemic has put me in the upside down. I'm underdressed. I should be wrapped in lights.

Grief or not, parades make me emotional. I'm crying, but not crying hard enough. I need to cry harder. I need to cry so hard I touch my own death and only then can I heal.

I've made a poster picturing my dead family members: my dog, my cousin, my father, my grandmother. I've used a picture of my dad before he was my dad. I found a picture of my grandma sitting at her desk at her job. She loved that job. I used a pic of my cousin smiling his big smile. I opened photo albums and pulled out more and more: my grandparents, my great-aunt and great-uncle, my great-grandparents. I glued the shit out of those pictures, afraid one might fall off. The poster board is big and flimsy and full. I carry that poster from Phoenix to downtown Tucson to the procession and back.

We're walking because we're alive. All of us. You and me and everyone here.

Acknowledgements

I AM GRATEFUL TO THE editors of the following pub-
lications, in which portions of this book first appeared,
sometimes in slightly different versions: *The Sun*, "Something
I Might Say"; *Autofocus Lit*, "Kill Floor"; and *Wigleaf*—who
offers all their writers the option of writing a postcard to run
along their flash pieces, which I took them up on. My "Dear
Wigleaf," now titled "All Souls," received a Mythic Picnic
Postcard Prize. Thank you, Andrew Snee, Michael Wheaton,
and Scott Garson.

My undying gratitude goes to Peg Alford Pursell, who has
encouraged me and supported me in this writing and helped
bring this full manuscript to light.

Thank you to Tod Goldberg, the first professional writer
who told me I could make it. I am forever grateful for that
hour he spent on the phone with me, and I swore if I ever was
fortunate enough to write book acknowledgements, I'd name
him near the top.

Thank you to Chelsey Clammer for being an early believer in my essays when I responded to a columnist call from *The Nervous Breakdown* in 2015 in a postpartum haze.

Thank you to Fred, my early Twitter #cnftweet crew.

I cannot say thank you hard enough to Liz Kay, my first and ideal reader. Her feedback is exactly what I always need, and more than a few times, she has pulled me off the floor and told me to keep going.

Thank you to the UNMFA program at the University of Nebraska-Omaha, specifically my fellow Firsters: Jen Lambert, Natalia Treviño, B.H. James, and Terry Kelly. Also, thank you to Ken Brosky and Sarah McKinstry-Brown and Gary Dop.

Thank you to the Sara Lippman workshop and all the writers inside: Julie Innis, Dan Sanders, Brendan Riley, Alice Kaltman, Josie Tolin, K.M. Rankey, and Lisa Trigg.

Thank you to mental health professionals, hospice nurses and volunteers, and nursing home staff. I owe you more than you know, and I promise to pay it forward.

Thank you to my friends and family and long-time supporters: Nicole Goodwin, Amy Vericker, Kate Tierney, and Kitty Austin.

I am indebted to journal editors and readers who donate their time to keep literature and the writing community going. Support your local independent literary journal and book press.

Thankful to my Grandma Sis, who supported me and my writing no matter how many swear words I used. She wished my first book would be a mystery but instead it's about her death, so not close, but I do hope she's proud of me wherever she is in the afterlife. Since this book was written, I've also lost my Great Aunt Gloria.

And hey, look at that family picture in 1985, the one where we were all dressed up as pirates: Mom, Dad, Me, Sister. We all wanted that family to survive, but it didn't, and all we could do was use the tools we had at the time. To my mother and sister, we've come a long way and I love you.

Finally, I am thankful for the family I have now: Mike, Blaze, and Cecilia (and our dog Holly, too), who make this hard fight called life worth living.

About the Author

[Photo credit: Lindsay McOien]

Stephanie Austin's short stories and essays have appeared in more than 25 literary journals and magazines including *The Sun, American Short Fiction, Autofocus Lit, Bending Genres, The Fiddlehead, Wigleaf, The Nervous Breakdown, The New England Review, Pithead Chapel, Carve Magazine, Pembroke Magazine,* and others. She has an MFA from the University of Nebraska-Omaha and is a 2012 Community of Writers Alum. She lives in Arizona with her husband, daughter, and high-strung dog. *Something I Might Say* is her debut book publication.

About WTAW Press

WTAW PRESS IS A 501(C)(3) nonprofit publisher devoted to discovering and publishing enduring literary works of prose. WTAW publishes and champions a carefully curated list of titles across a range of genres (literary fiction, creative nonfiction, and prose that falls somewhere in between), subject matter, and perspectives. WTAW welcomes submissions from writers of all backgrounds and aims to support authors throughout their careers.

As a nonprofit literary press, WTAW depends on the support of donors. We are grateful for the assistance we receive from organizations, foundations, and individuals. WTAW Press especially wishes to thank the following individuals for their sustained support.

Nancy Allen, Lauren Alwan, Robert Ayers, Andrea Barrett, Mary Bonina, Vanessa Bramlett, Harriet Chessman, Melissa Cistaro, Mari Coates, Kathleen Collison, Martha Conway, Michael Croft, Janet S. Crossen, R. Cathay Daniels, Ed Davis, Walt Doll, DB Finnegan, Joan Frank, Helen Fremont, Nancy Garruba, Michelle Georga, Ellen Geohegan, Anne Germanacos and the Germanacos Foundation, Rebecca Godwin, Stephanie Graham, Catherine Grossman, Teresa Burns Gunther, Annie Guthrie, Katie Hafner, Christine Hale, Jo Haraf, Adrianne Harun, Lillian Howan, Yang Huang, Joanna Kalbus, Caroline Kim-Brown, Scott Landers, Ksenija Lakovic, Evan Lavender-Smith, Jeffrey Leong, The Litt Family Foundation, Margot

Livesey, Karen Llagas, Nancy Ludmerer, Kevin McIlvoy, Jean Mansen, Sebastian Matthews, Grace Dane Mazur, Kate Milliken, Barbara Moss, Scott Nadelson, Betty Joyce Nash, Miriam Ormae-Jarmer, Cynthia Phoel, John Philipp, Lee Prusik, Gail Reitano, Joan Silber, Charles Smith, Michael C. Smith, Marian Szczepanski, Kendra Tanacea, Karen Terrey, Renee Thompson, Pete Turchi, Genanne Walsh, Judy Walz, Tracy Winn, Rebecca Winterer, Heather Young, Rolf Yngve, Olga Zilberbourg

To find out more about our mission and publishing program, or to make a donation, please visit wtawpress.org.

WTAW Press provides discounts and auxiliary materials and services for readers. Ebooks are available for purchase at our website book shop. Readers' guides are available for free download from our website. We offer special discounts for all orders of 5 or more books of one title.

Instructors may request examination copies of books they wish to consider for classroom use. If a school's bookstore has already placed an order for a title, a free desk copy is also available. Please use department letterhead when requesting free books.

Author appearances, virtual or in-person, can often be arranged for book groups, classroom visits, symposia, book fairs, or other educational, literary, or book events.

Visit wtawpress.org for more information.

WTAW Press
PO Box 2825
Santa Rosa, CA 95405
wtaw@wtawpress.org

Other titles available in print and ebook from WTAW Press

Promiscuous Ruins by Julian Mithra

Eggs in Purgatory by Genanne Walsh

Mississippi River Museum Keith Pilapil Lesmeister

One Kind Favor: A Novel by Kevin McIlvoy

The Groundhog Forever: A Novel by Henry Hoke

Like Water and Other Stories by Olga Zilberbourg

Chimerica: A Novel by Anita Felicelli

Hungry Ghost Theater: A Novel by Sarah Stone

Unnatural Habitats and Other Stories by Angela Mitchell

And There Was Evening and There Was Morning: A Memoir by Mike Smith

The Truth About Me: Stories by Louise Marburg